PILGRIM · GUIDE

✠

SALISBURY

Also available in the *Pilgrim Guide* series

PILGRIM · GUIDE

SALISBURY

Hugh Dickinson

Illustrated by Alison Jensen

CANTERBURY
PRESS
Norwich

Text © Hugh Dickinson 1997
Illustrations © Alison Jensen 1997

First published in 1997 by The Canterbury Press Norwich
(a publishing imprint of Hymns Ancient & Modern Limited
a registered charity)
St Mary's Works, St Mary's Plain
Norwich, Norfolk NR3 3BH

British Library Cataloguing in Publication Data

A catalogue record for this book is available
from the British Library

ISBN 1-85311-180-5

Typeset, printed and bound in Great Britain by
The Lavenham Press Ltd,
Lavenham, Suffolk, CO10 9RN

Contents

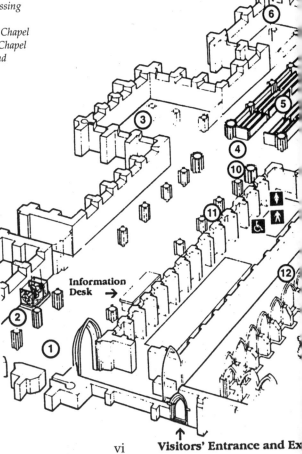

Information
Desk →

vi

Visitors' Entrance and Ex

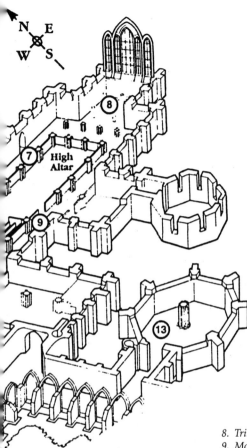

High Altar

View of Cathedral spire from Netherhampton

Introduction

This guide to Salisbury Cathedral is intended to help our visitors to discover a hidden dimension of this great building – a dimension which is not just history, heritage or architecture, but something more.

This hidden dimension is found in the response of the human spirit to a building which is not only ancient and beautiful but also deep. The Cathedral is more than 700 years deep; its roots go far down into the spiritual experience of many generations of English people and their awareness of God. It is still a sacred space where the presence of God can be felt and known today as it has been for centuries.

Among the hundreds of thousands of people who come here every year there are many who come with a conscious spiritual hunger. Some may already share the Christian faith with real conviction and come to worship; some may be 'seekers' who know the Christian story, but do not really know what they personally believe; others may have no religious faith at all, but are still looking for something – they don't quite know what – that seems to be missing. They are all pilgrims.

The religious symbolism of the Cathedral is Christian. Its present work and life is guided by the Christian tradition. But this guide can be used by anyone who simply wants to explore their own inner world of faith – whether they are Christian or humanist or nothing in particular. We hope that for them too it will open windows onto the world of the Spirit.

At the front of this book there is a plan of the Cathedral, with your pilgrim route mapped out for you.

The West End

We start at the West End of the Cathedral. Move into the centre of the Nave and stand just in front of the great West Doors. Stand quite still for a minute or two, and let the whole vista of the immense building open up in front of you and sink into your mind. You may like to sit in one of the chairs at the back of the Nave while you read.

✠

This strange and beautiful structure contains hidden within it many symbols and parables about the mystery of our human existence. In fact the whole of human life is held within this sacred space. To the observant eye and the attentive heart it presents images which offer answers to questions such as: What is the meaning of my life? Where is the world going? What lies beyond death? What guidance can I find for my pilgrimage through life?

Look up the length of the Nave. You will see there is not much colour. Everything is pointing upwards, as if inviting us to raise our eyes and lift our hearts to a different realm of being. Soft greys and browns and a wonderful succession of arcades lead your eyes up to a distant, half-hidden place and a dark-blue window at the far end of the Cathedral. When we get closer we will discover that in the central panel of the blue window the crucifixion of Christ is portrayed. That is the central image of the whole building. Even the ground-plan of the Cathedral is in the form of a cross. What does it mean?

Above the distant blue window there is another more brilliant one, higher and nearer, called the 'Moses Window'. In it is represented an incident from the Old Testament when the Jewish people were on pilgrimage through the Sinai desert. They were attacked by a plague of poisonous snakes whose bite was fatal. As they lie dying, Moses, their great prophetic leader, holds up before their eyes an immense golden snake twined around a cross-shaped staff. In the story, anyone who is bitten by a snake has only to look at the golden snake, and at once they are healed and saved.

So anyone who comes here asking, 'How can I be healed? How can I find a new life?' is offered an answer by these two images in these two stained-glass windows. Here is healing. Here is life. Yes, but how? Jesus said, 'I have come that you may have life and have it in all its abundance' (John 10:10).

Meditative prayer

I come here into this sacred space seeking a blessing from You, the Unseen Presence in this place. I come not knowing quite what I am seeking, not knowing who You are, or even knowing who I am myself. I come on pilgrimage, and as I walk through this sacred space for this short while, give me, Lord, a seeing eye and a listening heart. Let me discover something more of You and of myself before I leave.

Medieval Clock

The Medieval Clock

Now turn to your left and walk a few paces up the North Aisle on the far side of the row of pillars. On your left in an iron cage you will see an ancient clock. It's said to be the oldest mechanical clock still working in the world. It has no hands or face but only a great bell which chimes the hours of the day and night. With every slow swing of the escapement balance at the top, three seconds of time are chopped off our lives. There is something inexorable and frightening about this ancient machine. It has measured the life and death of so many hundreds of thousands of local people for over 600 years.

Look at the floor at your feet and you will see two small oblong paving slabs. These are the grave-markers of two sisters who died in childhood – Dorothy, aged five and her small sister Dolly, only nine months old.

On your right and on the stone bench between the pillars you will see the carved effigy of William Longspee, a great medieval nobleman. Nearby are the graves of Lord Wyndham and James, a tiny baby.

As you walk round the Cathedral you will see hundreds of other names on memorials and gravestones. They commemorate a multitude of human beings – men, women and children of all ages and all sorts.

A little further up on your left you will see hanging from flagpoles on the wall a row of ancient regimental 'colours'. These were the flags which soldiers used to carry into battle. Below them are lists of the regiments of men who were born and bred in this part of England, and who died in battle, often on the far side of the world. There is no distinction between the cowards and the heroes. Most of them died as young men who had not lived out half their lives. Both the heroism of war and also its brutality, waste and grief, which

William Longspee effigy

have clouded the lives of men and women in every generation, are also remembered here in this Cathedral.

All that sorrow and all those deaths are held in this sacred space long after the individual men and women have been erased from the conscious memory of the living. The ancient clock has ticked their lives away, and then their memory.

Except that those who knew and loved them brought their bones, or at least their names, into this holy place, as if they wanted to say to God: 'These were precious to us. We loved them. Let them be precious to You, even in death. They will soon be forgotten; let them be remembered in Your eternal love.'

Stand and listen to the clock for a few moments as it slowly ticks your life away. Look at the names and the carved figures. You may remember the verse of the hymn:

Time, like an ever-flowing stream,
Bears all its sons away.
They die forgotten as a dream
Fades at the opening day.

You may like to think of someone you know yourself who has recently died.

Death is the final enemy of humankind. But here there is a whisper of a hope that death does not have the last word.

Regimental Colours, North Side Aisle

Meditative prayer

Lord of Time, our short lives are passing shadows in the radiance of eternity, but You have made us for Yourself. Hold us in the hollow of Your hand, and when we in our turn go down into the dark, be there to hold us, even there, and gather us into Your love.

North Transept

Now walk up the North Aisle of the Nave, letting your eyes rest for a moment on the names and carved figures all around you. So many human beings! On the last pillar on the right hangs an embroidered tapestry of the Cathedral Spire pointing towards heaven. Under it are the words *Sursum Corda,* meaning 'Lift up your hearts!'

When you come to the North Transept you may like to wander round the Exhibition, which tells you something of the history of the building and its present use and life. You will see on one panel pictures of some of the many crosses which are to be seen in the building – again that central spiritual theme.

Through a narrow doorway in the carved screen on the far side of the Transept you can enter an enclosed side chapel. This is dedicated to St Edmund and St Thomas of Canterbury, two of the great holy men of England. On the screen behind you there are photographs of the Christian community in the Sudan, which is closely linked to this Cathedral. We keep their terrible tragedies in our hearts here every day and we link them in our prayers to the grace of God. Among them there are many great and holy people.

In this quiet space where you are away from all the other visitors, you may like to pause and sit for a few minutes to reflect on the astonishing achievement of this Cathedral. Look back and upwards into the main body of the building over the door through which you entered the Chapel. There you can see a miraculously beautiful vista of interlocking arcades and arches, woven together like silent music. Sit for a while and let it sing to you.

A Cathedral is a prodigious work of creative imagination; but it is also the product of sheer physical effort, the sweat and the manual skill of over 300 craftsmen and labourers who toiled continuously on the building for over 50 years. Every stone in these walls and arches was quarried, sawn, carved and polished by hand. Think of all those hands; think of the men working long hours in exhausting heat or freezing rain. They spent a whole lifetime of heavy labour on their craft to fashion this miracle in stone. Think also of the many others who laboured to support them – the quarrymen, the iron smelters, the woodsmen, the timber merchants, the charcoal burners, the herdsmen, the farmers, the tanners, the clothiers, and all their families. The life of the whole human community in this part of England was caught up and shaped by this prodigious enterprise.

Why did they do it? Well, of course, it was a job, and they were paid for it. But they were also driven by a profound religious urge to make something beautiful for God. The whole great edifice was meant to glorify the unseen God, like a hymn of praise in stone. It is a work of faith.

Look up at these soaring arches and see them as a kind of motionless dance or soundless music in honour of God. Four hundred feet above your head, on the tip of the spire, they set a bronze cross (you can see an earlier one on the far side of the transept). That too was a proclamation to the surrounding countryside that the glory of God was present in this place. People could get glimpses of the spire from the chalk downs ten miles away. It was a sign with powerful spiritual meaning. It spoke to them of healing, new life and life beyond death. They shared the deep religious faith of the builders.

And all down the centuries this Cathedral has been home to a great galaxy of saints and scholars and statesmen. St Edmund went on to become Archbishop of Canterbury. He would have been outstanding in any generation. Think of

Arches and Central vaulting

11

him sitting here 600 years ago, just where you are sitting. He was on pilgrimage like you. He followed a vision.

In our own age of doubt and cynicism it is difficult for us to recapture that vision. But it is still here waiting for us. Part of the purpose of this pilgrimage is to catch a glimpse of that vision.

Meditative prayer

Jesus said: 'Only believe and you will see the salvation of God.' Lord, open my ears to hear the silent music of this holy place; open my eyes to see the vision of glory which drew our forefathers to build it; let me glimpse in its beauty a shadow of that transcendent life which lies behind its outward material form. Lord, I do believe; help my unbelief.

The North Quire Aisle

When you are ready, walk back towards the centre of the Cathedral and turn left through the wrought-iron gates into the North Quire Aisle.

Beyond the organ case on the right you will see a 'cadaver tomb'. It may startle or even shock you to see this carving of a shrunken corpse. Of course, it was intended to shock. For this is the memorial of a great man who was famed for his intelligence, humour and goodness. He was Chaplain to Henry VII and Henry VIII. Now all that is left of him is a shrunken corpse. All, that is, except his spirit. It is as if from the grave he speaks to us across the centuries: 'Don't forget. You will be like this one day. Are you preparing your spirit for that final journey?' He died in absolute confidence in the promises of Jesus Christ. Jesus said: 'I am the Resurrection and I am Life. Anyone who dies believing in me will not ultimately die.'

Small doorway (Audley Chapel)

The Morning Chapel

Turn left through the doorway in the wooden screen on your left. Here you will find yourself in a side chapel which is partly divided into two spaces. On the right there is a stone font. This is used in the ceremony of Christian Baptism, when men, women or children are admitted into membership of the Christian Church. The family and friends of the candidates gather round the font as witnesses. The font is filled with water. The candidates are questioned about their belief and their understanding of the Christian faith. Then water is poured over their heads, as a sign of the washing away of a former way of life and the fresh beginning of a new life as a Christian, filled with God's own Spirit. Finally they are given a lighted candle as a symbol of the new light which is now at the centre of their lives. For many people this is where their Christian pilgrimage begins. Jesus said, 'I am the Light of the World.'

Behind the font you will see a modern embroidered panel. On each side is a large Greek letter – Alpha, the first letter of the Greek alphabet, and Omega, the last. They are symbols of Jesus Christ himself, who is the beginning and the end of the Christian life. They prompt us to reflect on the beginning and the end of our own lives: Where was I born? Where will I die?

The Christian faith believes that it is possible for human nature to be transformed. We do not have to go on living the way we do. Of course, many people have no desire to change their ways; they are quite content with things as they are. But there are many more who, consciously or unconsciously, are aware that things are not right with them. They may have things weighing on their conscience; they may just have a general sense of a deep hunger or a lack of meaning and direction in their lives.

You may at this point like to reflect on this present moment. It is the first moment of the rest of your life.

The symbol of the font reminds us that a new way of life is on offer. The choice is open to everyone. Millions of human beings have made that choice and have found that Jesus Christ is true to his promise: 'I am the Way, the Truth and the Life.'

Meditative prayer

Lord, sometimes, but not often, we are aware of another world, a world of the Spirit, just out of sight, beyond but also alongside or underneath the ordinary, everyday world. Just as the light falls into this holy place from these high windows, so glimpses of sunlight from that other world break in upon us with hints of joy and light which time cannot destroy. We feel an inner hunger for that other way of life. If You are the Way, show me the way I should walk in; if You are the Truth, lead me away from shadows to reality; if You are the Life, let my small spirit be drawn in to Your Eternal Spirit.

The Trinity Chapel

Now leave the Chapel and turn left up the aisle. Ahead of you there is a window dedicated to George Herbert, behind a rather absurd sixteenth-century tomb. You can see him pictured in his black gown on the left of the window. Herbert was the much-loved parish priest of the small church at Bemerton, two miles west of the Cathedral. (There is a quiet walk across the water-meadows to his tiny church, which is still standing.) He was also one of the finest poets in the English language. One of his best-known poems is printed on p. 23.

Move on into the chapel at the East End of the Cathedral. There is much to see and much for a pilgrim to think about in this chapel. You may like to sit and look around you for a while.

The great blue window is the most striking feature of this chapel. It was made in the glass-works at Chartres in France and was installed in 1980. It is dedicated to prisoners of conscience all over the world. (The chapel is used as a national shrine by Amnesty International; the rough wrought-iron Amnesty candle stands to the left of the altar.)

Take some time to study the window. Except in the early morning, when the sun shines directly onto it, it is quite mysterious and dark. In the central panel is the figure of the crucified Christ. Below him on the left is the half-hidden figure of his mother, the Blessed Virgin Mary, her head covered by a blue hood and bowed in sorrow.

Above the head of Christ a shower of gold touches the top of the window. From him a broad triangle of lighter blue strikes down into the darker glass at the left-hand side. In the panels on either side you can discern dozens of other faces and heads. These are the prisoners of conscience of

Amnesty candlestick, Trinity Chapel

every nation. Some have crosses among them, signifying that these are Christian prisoners; but many others have just jagged daggers of glass. These are the martyrs of conscience of all lands and all faiths.

Down into their dark and tortured world the light of Christ on the Cross penetrates. It's as if God is saying to them, 'Do not despair. I too have known the same imprisonment, the same torture, the same awful death. You are not forgotten. Justice and mercy will prevail. The resurrection of Christ from the dead is my promise that death and evil do not have the last word.' The hint of that resurrection glory is visible in the golden glass at the top of the window. It is only a hint, but it is there.

The Altar

Below the window there is a wide Altar Table. Early every morning on every day of the year the staff of the Cathedral gather here to celebrate the Eucharist at this Altar. The Eucharist is celebrated to represent the Last Supper of Jesus with his disciples and to commemorate his crucifixion and resurrection. That is the power-house of the Christian religion. It represents God taking the pain and sin and fatal inhumanity of our human race to himself and breaking its hold on us. The huge spiritual power of Christianity down the centuries flows from the Cross. It has transformed the lives of hundreds of millions of men, women and children.

In front of the Altar is a remarkable embroidered frontal. At first sight it appears to be an abstract modern painting. But, as we focus our eyes on it, it resolves itself into the sky-line of a modern city, with skyscrapers over city streets. It might be New York or Tokyo, Brazilia or the City of London. It represents modern urban society, with its extremes of wealth and abject poverty, its violence and its technological achievement, its rich culture and its human degradation. You might imagine the Last Supper taking place behind one of those lighted windows in one of those skyscrapers.

Above it in the blue window hangs the crucified Christ. He carries all that pain and poverty – the drug addicts, the abused children, the wasted and corrupted lives. God's love is still crucified in the cruelty of the modern world. It's a strange paradox: so much pain in such a beautiful window. Here in this sacred space we hold both the beauty and the pain of the world. We have to hold them together, because without the pain the beauty has no heart, and without the beauty the pain has no hope.

But the promise in the window and in the altar frontal is

Candlestick on High Altar

the same. Christ is doing something to rescue us from the despair and darkness of the world. There is a great stream of healing and life which flows from him into the hearts and lives of those who open themselves to his light. They in turn can become sources of healing and love to others.

If you look closely at the figure of Christ in the centre of the blue window, you will see that under each of his out-stretched arms there is a chalice or cup. From the wounds in his hands drops of his blood are falling into each chalice.

Early each morning on every day of the year a chalice just like that is placed on the Altar here, and with it a piece of bread. Members of the Cathedral staff and the community gather round in worship. They thank God for the beauty of his world and for the revelation of his love. They read out passages from the Bible. They pray for the whole human race, especially for those who are suffering in the cruel and dark places of the world.

Then the priest blesses the bread and the wine in the chalice, and they are shared out among all who are present.

This Communion service is one of the most ancient of all religious rites. The bread has been blessed and broken and the wine has been blessed and shared like this for nearly two thousand years by Christ's people all over the world. It establishes and renews in them a personal communion with him, and through him with the mystery of God himself. The bread and wine are vehicles of his grace and presence. Then the worshippers go out into their daily work, empowered by his Spirit to live as agents of his Kingdom and instruments of his love.

Here is a poem by George Herbert in which he pictures the Lord inviting him to sit at his table and receive the holy bread and wine:

Love bade me welcome, yet my soul drew back,
Guilty of dust and sin.
But quick-eyed Love, observing me grow slack
From my first entrance in,
Drew near to me, sweetly questioning
If I lacked anything?

'A guest', I answered, 'worthy to be here.'
Love said, 'You shall be he.'
'I, the unkind, ungrateful? Ah, my dear
I cannot look on Thee.'
Love took my hand and, smiling, did reply,
'Who made the eyes, but I?'

'Truth, Lord, but I have marred them. Let my shame
Go where it doth deserve.'
'And know you not,' says Love, 'Who bore the blame?'
'My dear, then I will serve.'
'You must sit down,' says Love, 'and taste my meat.'
So I did sit and eat.

It may be that as you sit in this serene and beautiful place, some of your own griefs and the painful things in your own life will come to the surface of your mind. People quite often find themselves weeping here, whether for themselves, for some friend or relative, or for the pain and the waste of so many human lives. Thinking about all that pain makes it hard to believe in God at all. Perhaps it's only here, in front of the crucified Christ, who is called the Son of God, that it is emotionally possible to believe, because he is in the midst of all the pain too.

Meditative prayer

Lord, sometimes the darkness and suffering of the world seems overwhelming. There is so much pain and grief, so much senseless waste, that it is hard to believe that there is any future to hope for, or even to believe that You exist. Yet, loving Father, I want to believe; I want to hope. I want to stand for truth and freedom and justice and peace. Let the light of Christ's love penetrate this anxious heart of mine. Help me to believe that in the end You will rescue, heal and transform me and all the countless people of our human race.

Mary the Mother of Jesus

Before you leave the chapel, look to your left and you will see a charming little wooden image of Our Lady, the Virgin Mary, the mother of Jesus, carved somewhere in France in the fifteenth century. In her arms she carries the infant Christ, her first-born son, who is going to end up tortured to death on the Cross thirty years later. Think of her heartbreak, and think of the endless weeping of all the mothers who have seen their children imprisoned, tortured or executed down the centuries. All their grief is held by her in this holy place.

As you leave, stop for a moment beside one of the slender Purbeck marble columns which hold up the vaulting of the roof. If you look closely you will see that in the marble there are hundreds of little paler flecks and particles. These are the fossilized shells of the tiny sea creatures which lived in the warm seas which once covered this land. Over many hundreds of millions of years their remains became a sediment on the sea-bed, in places hundreds of feet deep. As it was compacted over the ages, it formed the hard limestones and marbles which are the underlying rocks of this part of England. We think of this Cathedral as an ancient building, but in geological time these little sea creatures are almost infinitely older, far older than the Alps or the Himalayas. Even they are not all that old in the life-span of this planet, and the planet itself not so very old in comparison with cosmic time. In all those inconceivable aeons of time, the Creator God was at work in his universe, planning, moulding, guiding and waiting.

Waiting for the appearance of a creature who could know him and respond to him. That is what this great building is for. A place in the middle of infinite time and unimaginable

Carved Madonna and Child, Trinity Chapel

space where tiny human beings can respond to the great, mysterious Presence which we call God. He holds all time and all space in his hands. And, perhaps, right from the beginning, there was a Cross in the heart of God.

The Prickett Stand

Leave the Trinity Chapel on the opposite side from where you came in. Immediately on your left you will see a stand for votive candles in front of one of the most magnificent memorials in the Cathedral. It records one of the great noble dynasties of Tudor times. But in the embrasure to the right you will see the reproduction of an ancient Byzantine ikon of the head of Christ. There is a strange dissonance between the grandiloquence of all those noble coats of arms and this simple but deeply moving portrait of Jesus.

But here visitors from all over the world always pause. They give only a glance to the gilded splendour of the tomb, but many often stand still to look into the eyes of Christ or kneel before him to say a prayer.

Every year thousands of people come to light a candle here. For many it is an unspoken prayer for a loved one who is far away, or for a friend or relative who is in trouble or has died. Some light a candle for themselves and leave it to burn here before the face of Christ. Others light a candle for the Sudan or Rwanda or Bosnia, or for all the children of the world. One young couple lit a candle for the unborn baby they had just lost.

For several hours after pilgrims have left, their little flame of prayer will continue to burn here. It is a thread of gold which links them to God and to those for whom they pray.

You may like to kneel here for a moment and to look into the face of Christ. Before you leave, light a candle for someone you love – or for yourself. It will still be burning here long after you have left. We may forget God. He never forgets us.

South Quire Aisle

Now walk to your left down the South Quire Aisle. About ten paces down on the wall on your left you will see a brass memorial to a great nineteenth-century Christian scholar called Henry Liddon. Towards the bottom of the engraved inscription you will see these words:

> His writings will in part reveal to those who come after his subtle genius, his ready wit, his grace and learning, but only those who mourn him and miss his help know the brightness of his living presence.

That is just a little echo from the past of the power of Christ's Spirit to mould and transform our human nature and to make men and women who are so gracious, generous and good. Henry Liddon must have been a truly lovely man. What made him so? And where has all that human goodness and genius gone? Is it just extinguished, like a candle being blown out?

Continue on down the aisle and through the wrought-iron gateway at the end. Turn to your left and pass the two open chapels on your left, until you come to the doorway into the third small chapel. Turn in (mind the step!) Look up to your right at the stained glass window. In the left-hand panel is a portrayal of the crucifixion of Christ. In the right-hand panel is the resurrection.

St Michael's Chapel

It is an odd feature of this Cathedral that this is its only really striking representation of the resurrection of Jesus Christ from the dead. (There is a fine Christ in Glory in the north window in the Morning Chapel.) It's almost as if it is a secret which is so strange and momentous that you have to go and search for it.

This is the most tremendous secret contained in this building. For if the resurrection had not happened, there would be no Cathedral and no Christian faith. The power of the first Christians to convert the Gentile world was generated by their encounter with the risen Christ. His apparent failure and terrible death was not the last word. Out of that tragic ending sprang this fountain of new spiritual life and energy, which has changed the world and has transformed the lives of millions of people down the centuries.

There are no absolute proofs of the resurrection of Jesus. What actually happened on the first Easter morning is shrouded in conflicting evidence and confusion. But the indisputable evidence that something momentous and extraordinary did happen is the resulting explosion of spiritual power into human affairs all down the centuries and the witness of millions upon millions of transformed human lives. This building and all that goes on in it is a modern witness to the empty tomb 2,000 years ago.

In the corner of the chapel you will see a small red lamp burning. That is a sign that behind the curtain in the wall some of the sacramental bread from the Holy Eucharist is secretly reserved. Christians have always believed that the sacramental bread symbolizes and carries the living presence of the risen Christ. Sit quite still for a moment in this small chapel. Close your eyes and breathe deeply and calmly. Let the sense of his secret Presence begin to soak into your consciousness. All you need to say is, 'Lord, You are here – I wait for You to touch my soul.'

✠

Meditative prayer

Lord, like Your friend Thomas, who doubted Your resurrection, I find it hard to believe that You really are here. I find it hard to believe that You really did pass through death and out the other side. But You promised that You would be with us until the end of time. Open my spirit now to a new awareness of Your living reality. Touch my cold and anxious heart with the warmth and energy of Your personal love. Kindle in me a living faith in Your presence and Your power. Let me know something of the joy which Your first disciples found when they met You on that far-off Easter morning.

Under the Crossing

When you leave St Michael's Chapel turn to your right again and walk back to the centre of the Cathedral. Stand under the Crossing for a moment. This is the central axis of the Cathedral, where the arms of the cross which is its ground-plan intersect with the upright. Immediately above you is the soaring spire. Here at the centre of the building there is usually a great lectern with a copy of the Bible open on it. You may like to go up the steps behind the lectern and read a few words from the text, wherever it happens to have been opened. People sometimes find that a few words leap out of the page and catch their eye as if personally addressed to them.

The Bible

The Bible is the sacred book of the Christian Church. In fact it is a collection of books gathered together in two unequal parts over a period of perhaps a thousand years, dealing with events of twice that time-span. It contains history, myth, poetry, legislation, prophecy, personal letters and visionary dreams The first part (the Old Testament) is the Jewish Scriptures. The second part (the New Testament) – much the shorter – deals with the life and ministry of Jesus Christ and the subsequent experiences of his first disciples in the first century AD.

For Christians this is the Holy Book. It tells of the dealings of God with generation after generation of men and women who have tried to serve and worship him. But it also contains God's messages and commandments. More

Pulpit in Main Crossing

important than all, it contains the actual words of Jesus Christ and eyewitness accounts of his actions.

Christians believe that in Christ's words and actions we encounter the mind and purpose of God himself, translated into human language. These words have immense power to penetrate deep into the hearts and minds of people of every age, culture and society and to transform and inspire their lives.

Christians often say that the Bible is 'inspired by God'. Sometimes they think that must mean that every word is absolutely true and accurate. But perhaps it makes more sense to say that because it is inspired by God, Scripture has an extraordinary power to touch and change human lives – to speak straight to the heart of every man, woman or child, whatever their circumstances or background.

As you stand here, spend a moment reflecting what a profound influence this book has had on the history of two millennia. It has been translated into almost every known human language, and among primitive peoples it has often been the first written document in their language. It has been carried into the jungles of South America and the deserts of central Africa to the South Pole with Captain Scott and to the remotest islands of the Pacific with Captain Cook.

It was secretly treasured in the Nazi concentration camps. It has been publicly displayed at the crowning of Emperors and the swearing in of Presidents. Nelson Mandela read it in his prison on Robbin Island, and he still reads it as the South African Head of State.

It is placed beside the beds in almost every hotel in the civilized world, and it is carried in the briefcases of hundreds of thousands of business people. Men and women have been prepared to die for it. It has been studied more closely and commented on more extensively by scholars than any other human text. Until recently, every home in this country from the poorest to the most wealthy would have treasured a family Bible.

Whether we know it or not, the words of this book have shaped our own minds and thoughts in profound and subtle ways. Its images and stories resonate in our memories and colour the way we think about ourselves. In a dark, mysterious universe, and in an often meaningless world, it has offered the human race light, purpose and meaning. It tells us that human history has a destination and that every individual human life can share in that destiny and find fulfilment in pursuing it.

Meditative prayer

Lord, this is a dark and mysterious universe. For thousands of years our ancestors struggled to make sense of their lives in the midst of its strange beauties and terrible pains. Now You have shown us in Your Word the true meaning of our lives. In Jesus a great shaft of sunlight has come into our clouded world. In him You have set before our eyes a model of what it is to be both human and divine. Let a glimpse of this light touch and illuminate my own darkness and confusion and uncertainty. Speak to me from Your Word the words of peace and love. Lead me into Your truth.

The Quire

Now turn back towards the east and walk up the centre of the Cathedral between the choir stalls. In a way this is the engine room of the Cathedral. Along the back on each side you will see a long row of seats or stalls with elaborate carved canopies over them. These are the seats where the Canons and clergy of the Cathedral sit for the daily services of worship. At the four corners are the seats of the four 'Principal Persons' or senior clergy who are responsible for the governance of the Cathedral. Above on both sides are the serried ranks of organ pipes. Right in the middle are the choir stalls with their brass lamps.

Here you can see the whole purpose or *raison d'être* of the Cathedral – the offering of daily worship and praise and prayer to God. Except for a period of a few weeks during the Civil War in the seventeenth century worship has been offered here every single day for over 700 years.

The form which the worship takes varies from time to time, but is always essentially the same – the singing of psalms and canticles and the reading of passages of Scripture.

Because God is himself the source of all beauty and holiness, nothing but the best will do in our offering to him. So the organ and the music which it provides are of the very finest. So is the singing by skilled musicians and highly trained boys and girls. Everything we do has to be an echo or reflection of the glory of God , so it has to be as beautiful as we can make it.

It is worth spending some time looking at the fine carvings on some of the stalls. You can find angels with musical instruments, strange animals, and leaf and flower forms. It's as if these carvings are saying to us that the whole of creation takes part in the worship which we offer to God.

Carved Angels, Choir Stalls

God's glory permeates his universe – not only the stars and nebulae in distant space, but also the birds and insects and micro-organisms of our planet. The beauty of the parakeets in the Amazon jungles or of the white tigers in India is a reflection of God's beauty too.

But only our human race can offer articulate and conscious worship to God our Creator. So we have to do it on behalf of the whole of creation as well.

This is part of one of the canticles which the Choir regularly sings here:

> O all ye works of the Lord, bless ye the Lord,
>> Praise him and magnify him for ever.
> O ye angels of the Lord, bless ye the Lord,
>> Praise him and magnify him for ever.
> O ye Sun and Moon, bless ye the Lord,
> O ye stars of heaven, bless ye the Lord,
> O ye showers and dew, bless ye the Lord,
>> Praise him and magnify him for ever.
> O ice and snow, bless ye the Lord,
> O lightnings and clouds, bless ye the Lord,
> O let the Earth bless the Lord,
>> Praise him and magnify him for ever.
> O seas and floods, bless ye the Lord,
> O whales and all that move in the waters, bless ye the Lord,
> O all ye beasts and cattle, bless ye the Lord,
>> Praise him and magnify him for ever.
> O ye children of men, bless ye the Lord,
> O ye servants of the Lord, bless ye the Lord,
> O spirits and souls of the righteous, bless ye the Lord,
>> Praise him and magnify him for ever.

Why do we do it? To keep open and make explicit the

channels of grace and love between God and the human community and the creatures of the natural world in which we live.

Worship is offered here not only for the natural world but for the whole of human society, particularly for those who never pray themselves or have no religious faith or spiritual awareness of any kind.

This space is a kind of spiritual telephone exchange. We reach out in our compassion and prayers to all the painful and dark places of the world where humanity is suffering appalling pains and griefs; and then we reach out to God in all his mercy and glory, opening ourselves as channels of his grace into his world.

This task of keeping open the reality of the world of the Spirit is the chief function of the Cathedral, and one which is possibly more urgently needed today than at any other time in its history. Every day, as new babies are being born and old people are going to their last rest, the steady and unfailing heart-beat of our daily worship brings each new generation of the human community into contact with the radiation of the Divine Love and commends the dead and dying to his mercy. That is what it is all for.

Meditative prayer

Lord, You have made a strange and beautiful world full of echoes of Your glory. Open our senses to an awareness of the world of the Spirit which underlies and enfolds all things. Fill our hearts with such wonder that they are full of praise as well. Let my small spirit join in the great hymn of praise which ascends to You from all created things. Widen my sympathies and make my response to all creatures deeper and more generous, so that I may walk through the world greeting that which is of God in every thing and every one.

The Presbytery

Walk up the step towards the Sanctuary and the High Altar. On your right you will see the Bishop's Chair. It is very grand and ornate and is surmounted by a pinnacle of carved wood. You may like to sit in one of the chairs at the side while you read on.

The Cathedral is the Mother Church of the Diocese, the area which is administered by the Bishop. In this case the Diocese of Salisbury covers the two counties of Wiltshire and Dorset, with over 300 parish churches. The Bishop is the Chief Pastor and he has his *cathedra* or chair here – hence the name 'Cathedral'.

Down the centuries the Christian Church has extended its reach across the world by sending out missionary Bishops with authority to found new local communities of Christians, to teach them the Christian faith and to help them build places of worship. There is an unbroken line of authorization of the Bishops of the Church right back to the first century. You can see the long list of Bishops of Salisbury carved in a marble plaque at the West End of the Cathedral. Beyond them the personal human link goes right back through the early Church and the first disciples, back to Jesus himself.

The first Bishop of Salisbury was the great St Osmund in the eleventh century AD. He was a famous scholar, an outstanding administrator and a fine musician. His first Cathedral was built two miles to the north of the present building, inside the walls of a massive Norman castle at Old Sarum. (The site is still well worth visiting.)

Osmund founded the choir school, which is still flourishing today. Many of his books are still treasured in the Cathedral Library. He was a man of great holiness and had a reputation for a gift of healing, which brought many sick people here during his lifetime. After his death thousands came to visit his shrine in the hope that his sanctity would still effect a cure for their ailments. Sadly, his shrine was destroyed during the Reformation, but you can see part of it in the South Aisle of the Nave.

Today the Cathedral still preserves the tradition of Osmund's healing powers by holding regular healing services. Once a month forty or fifty people gather to pray for healing for themselves or their friends, and they receive the laying on of hands with prayer. It is a sign of God's continuing grace here that many of them do find relief and comfort and a new energy for life through this ministry.

You may like to sit or kneel here for a few minutes and to reflect on the things in your own life which need healing – the wounds and griefs which we all experience on our journey through life. There may be heavy things on our consciences or memories which bring back a sense of guilt. Here it is possible to bring them to God and to ask his forgiveness and healing.

And it may be there is some particular person for whom we want to ask a blessing. This place is a power-house of prayer, and all our little prayers, however faltering, are caught up in the constant stream of prayer which is offered before the throne of God every day. Your prayer can be carried on that stream. (You could go back and light a candle, if you wish to at this point.)

Meditative prayer

. . . More things are wrought by prayer
Than this world dreams of. Wherefore let thy voice
Rise like a fountain for me night and day.
For what are men better than sheep or goats
That nourish a blind life within the brain,
If, knowing God, they lift not hands of prayer
Both for themselves and for those who call them friend?
For so the whole round earth is every way
Bound by gold chains about the feet of God.

Tennyson

The Sanctuary and the High Altar

Now move up a further step to the Communion Rail, which acts as a boundary to the Sanctuary. Ahead of you in the centre of the open space at the top of a further flight of steps is the High Altar. This is the climax of our pilgrimage round the building. Here every Sunday the Eucharist is celebrated with great solemnity for the large congregation which gathers for worship. The whole community is represented here.

The Altar is in fact a table on which the bread and wine are blessed. The congregation is reminded of the Last Supper of Jesus on the night before he was executed, when he sat down with his disciples and blessed the bread and the wine for them to share with him. It was a solemn meal full of foreboding for his terrible death the next day. But it also carried a sense of destiny and a promise of a strange glory. For Jesus pictured the life beyond death as a great festival, when God will gather in all his sons and daughters from all times and all places and seat them at a banquet. Then all tears will be wiped from their eyes, all their wounds will be healed and all their injustices will be remedied.

When Christ's people gather here Sunday by Sunday they look back to the Last Supper of Jesus with his friends 2,000 years ago; but they are also looking forward to that great heavenly banquet beyond the end of time. Sharing in the bread and wine is for them a foretaste of the joy of heaven. That is our destiny, however clouded and painful our present life may be. Just as Jesus Christ looked forward to that new life beyond his own execution, so by absorbing his life now his followers come to share his vision, and to live with an entirely new perspective.

When we began this short pilgrimage we noticed how many memorials there are here of the dead from past generations. Now perhaps we can begin to understand why. All those lost and incomplete lives are not utterly lost. In his own time – at the end of time – God will gather them all up into his arms: the saints and scholars, the children and soldiers, the housewives and farmers, the Bishops and vagabonds, the labourers and earls. Their bodies have decayed to dust and bones under the paving of this holy place or under the turf in the Churchyard outside it. Death is the final enemy of humankind, but death does not have the last word. The last word is God's, who says, 'Behold, I make all things new!'

The South Nave Aisle

We have now reached the climax of our pilgrimage, but there is still much to see and reflect on. You can now find your way back towards the West End of the Cathedral.

Retrace your steps to the central Crossing. There turn left and then right into the South Nave Aisle. On your right you will see part of the dismantled tomb of St Osmund. In medieval times pilgrims came here seeking healing from the Saint for their ills and ailments, and there are a number of historical records of people being healed. Pilgrims would place their sick children – or their own arms or legs – inside the apertures in the tomb to get as close to the bones of the Saint as possible. You can see how the marble round the holes in the base is polished and discoloured by the constant wear of human limbs.

Further down on the left there is a fascinating model of the Cathedral in the process of being built. You can get some idea of the heaviness of the labour and the complexity of the task. But the model can give you no inkling of the intensity of the faith of all those forgotten craftsmen and labourers who spent their lives making this immense hymn of praise in stone.

Beyond the model on the wall by the doorway there is the long list of Bishops of Salisbury. It gives us some sense of the continuity of the community of faith here.

Before you leave the Cathedral you may like to go back and stand once more at the place where you first stood when you entered, just in front of the great West Doors. In imagination you can picture this huge space empty of all chairs.

Imagine that the West Doors are open onto a bright June morning on some great festival day in the fifteenth century.

Organ pipes (Willis Organ)

Through them comes a procession, headed by the Cross and candles, followed by the Choir singing plainsong, and then the clergy, the Canons and the Dean in the finest brilliant robes, with acolytes swinging incense in golden censers. Finally, gorgeously arrayed, comes the Bishop in his high mitre, accompanied by his chaplains and attendants. Behind him a long procession of townsfolk and labourers, of nobles and yeomen comes flooding into the shadows of the Cathedral.

The whole solemn array passes up through the Cathedral to the far end for devotions at the shrine of St Osmund. You can hear the plainsong chants echoing in the distance. You can almost feel the atmosphere of awe and faith which so moved the hearts of those long-ago Christian people.

But you don't have to stretch your imagination to recapture that far-off world of faith. You can experience it as a living reality in the modern world. There are many occasions in the year when the Cathedral is packed to the doors with over 2,000 worshippers. People come from all over the world to attend the services at the Great Festivals of Christmas and Easter, Advent and Pentecost. The music and singing is more glorious than it has ever been in any previous age. The worship is as profound and moving as it was in medieval times.

Imagine this great space full of worshippers at the Midnight Eucharist last Christmas. There are 2,500 people here. In spite of the vast crowd there is utter silence, as if every single person present were holding their breath to hear the silent music of the building itself, and to catch the tingling sense that in the midst of them there is a palpable Presence which is the Presence of God himself.

That sense of the numinous – the unseen Presence of God in the midst – can be experienced at almost any service in the

Cathedral, whether it is the quiet early morning worship, or the crowded Sunday services, or Choral Evensong on a bitter winter night, when there are no more than a dozen people present, apart from the clergy and Choir praying and singing in the soft lamplight. Even then the place feels as if it is full of angels.

If you have never experienced that sense of the present Holiness of God, it would be worth making the effort to travel even a long journey to meet it. Many people have had their lives transformed by that experience.

At the far end of the Cathedral turn left out of the door, pass through the little vestibule (which used to be an ecclesiastical court) and out into the Cloister beyond.

The Cloister

If it is fine you may like to wander round the Cloister and reflect quietly on what you have experienced in your pilgrimage round the Cathedral. Here you are beginning to get back into the everyday world, and this quiet time spent walking round this green and peaceful place can make a bridge between the two worlds which we inhabit.

This is the largest Cloister in England. It was designed partly as a processional way for use in wet weather, but partly as a sheltered and serene space for reflection. As you walk you are treading on flagstones where generation after generation of men and women have quietly paced to think about their lives.

The two worlds we inhabit are not really separate realms. The world of the Spirit underlies our everyday working world and penetrates it in all sorts of secret and unnoticed ways. Making a pilgrimage round an ancient Cathedral helps us to get back in touch with this hidden world and with a part of ourselves that is often starved and thirsty.

Here there are hidden springs of water just under the surface. These great cedar trees flourish here by putting down their roots into the underlying water in the deep bed of gravel underground. Many people feel that their lives are arid and dried up for want of spiritual nurture. God is the Well of Life. Our spirits flower and grow when we put down roots into his deep Spirit.

As you walk slowly round, think about the life you are going back to. What nurtures it? Where does it feel arid? What is your heart's desire? Where will you draw water to refresh your spirit? In this place, what is the Holy Spirit whispering to you?

The secret Presence which you have encountered here is

Cloisters

waiting for you at home, in your relationships, in your work, in your loves – yes, and in your pains and griefs. The Divine Love holds and enfolds you, whether you know it or not. How can you put down fresh roots into that life-giving stream ?

Meditative prayer

> Drop thy still dews of quietness,
> Till all our strivings cease.
> Take from our souls the stress,
> And let our ordered lives confess
> The beauty of thy peace.

The Walking Madonna

We have not quite finished, however. When you leave the Cloister by the door that leads onto the West Front of the Cathedral, turn right and walk a hundred yards up the path which leads into the city.

On your right you will see a bronze statue by Elisabeth Frink. It is a portrait of Mary, the Mother of Jesus in old age, striding out towards the busy rush and hum of the city outside the Close. You can see the grief and hardship of her life etched in her face, but she is full of energy and determination.

Before you leave, stand beside her for a moment. You are walking out into your everyday life. Perhaps she has something to say to you that you need to hear. Perhaps you can tell her what it is you are taking with you from the Cathedral. Putting it into words is a way of making sure that you keep it and do not let it be erased and lost by the rush and busyness of your everyday life.

Go with God. God goes with you.

'Walking Madonna' (Elisabeth Frink)

Pilgrimage to Salisbury

We come, Lord, from arid lands,
parched by the dust and heat
of this relentless world, to this field
where five waters meet. We bring
nothing in our hands except
these gestures of prayer and a void
where the heart should be.
We aren't sure why we have come,
or what we seek. Is it to rest
under these willows? Is it for these meadows
and clear waters, to lie in the tall grasses
under the humming sun, and dream?
To forget that the world is hard and grey,
just for one hour? Is it to find
a ford where the dust and pain
can be washed and soothed in the bright
chalk stream? To watch the brown trout loiter
there in the deep by the shingle bank?
Or is it to find a wooden bridge to cross,
built by a priest or carpenter to hold
this world to the beyond, so that our feet
may make spiritual transition?
Is it for this we come?
Or did we come to satisfy some
other hunger, heal some more ancient pain?
Pass on, pass over. Within the five wounds
of these streams there lies a silence,
a still space where the air waits
and is still. It waits for you.

Yes, take off your shoes. Let the stream
wash your feet. She has knelt here for 700 years
waiting for you to come.
Yes, bend and drink the clear water. It is for you.
Salute the fish. It is His sentinel,
His countersign. Lie in the summer grass; it is your flesh
and must die with the first frosts.
Let it dream. Then pass on, pass over.
The darkness waits, as does the silence.

Well, what shall we say, now we are here?
The old words will do as well as any, the old songs:
Kyrie, Kyrie, Kyrie eleison.

Now is the time of silence. No words now,
no music. Pick up your candle – you
are this small flame – it is your angel
under the high vault among the pillars and shadows
of the aisles. Walk in a whisper. Greet
the dead, the many gathered dead whose
candles burn now on the further shore;
and as you pass, summon them by name,
to pray for you. And pray for them
Kyrie, Kyrie, Kyrie eleison.

Now at last under the central cross
enter the circle. This ring of lights
is drawn by that one still central flame.
Stand still.
Be empty.
Wait.
Beneath your feet the roots of this silence
reach down beyond the centre of the Earth

into the abyss of God. Hold fast your angel.
Stand on the brink of that unfathomable chasm.
Be still.
Be empty.
Let God be God.
Listen and wait. Let his mysterious love
do his own secret work within your emptiness.
It is for this emptiness you came.

Now it is time to go. Leave
your small candle in the shadow of this aisle.
Part of you stays here. Say farewell.
Greet the Angel of the Place with love,
then walk out into the dusk
of the ordinary day. Re-cross the stream,
the sleeping meadow and the watchful fish.
Journey home. And before you sleep
greet with quiet joy the flame that
burns at the central crossing
of your inner silent space.
Then sleep.

Hugh Dickinson